STAND WOMAN STAND! 3RD EDITION

~FAITH IT!~

A COMPILATION OF POETIC PIECES

By: Valerie Golden Allen
&
Guest Poets

™Stand Woman Stand! 3rd Edition
By: Valerie Golden Allen

Published by:
VJ PUBLISHINGHOUSE, LLC.
20451 NW 2nd Avenue Suite112 Miami Gardens, Fl. 33169
 Phone:786-535-9598
www.vjpublishinghouse.com
vjpublishinghouse@gmail.com

©Copyright: 2023, October
All Rights Reserved:
No portion of this book or any digital products may be reproduced, stored, in any retrieval system, or transmitted by any means without the written consent of Publisher/Authors except in reviews or articles with Author and Publisher consent or as permitted by U.S. copyright law.

 ISBN#: 978-1-939236-20-3 (Paperback)

Because of you **WOMAN**,
I have the courage to **'STAND!'**

Valerie Golden Allen

In Loving Memory of

~Mama~

Juanita Brockington Golden
9/9/1932 – 8/11/2021

Mama, you always made time to listen
You spoke just what I needed to hear
You inspired me to reach higher
To **'STAND'** and **Persevere**

On the days when I stumbled
You extended your hand so I wouldn't fall
With your steadfast faith and courage
Your **LOVE** covered it **'ALL'**

Because of you, I am stronger, wiser, and most of all better…

Miss you Mama

'Roe'

YOU WILL ARISE AND HAVE COMPASSION
ON ZION, FOR IT IS TIME
TO SHOW FAVOR TO HER
THE APPOINTED TIME HAS COME

PSALMS 102:13

CONTENTS

Introduction — 1

Chapter 1 — 2

Chapter 2 — 18

Chapter 3 — 32

Chapter 4 — 50

Chapter 5 - Guest Poets — 62

Special Tribute to Women/ From A Man's Perspective — 93

Closing Signature Piece — 98

A Special Invitation — 102

Contact Information — 103

~INTRODUCTION~

WOMAN, DO YOU KNOW WHO YOU ARE?
DO YOU UNDERSTAND YOU WERE CREATED WITH A PURPOSE?
ARE YOU WONDERING WHY YOU ARE EVEN HERE?
WELL, GOD HAS HOPES AND BLESSINGS FOR YOU.
BEFORE YOU WERE CREATED IN YOUR MOTHER'S WOMB,
HE HAD IN HIS MIND
ALL THE PURPOSES FOR YOUR LIFE CYCLE.
ALTHOUGH THERE HAS BEEN SOME BUMPS
AND BENDS ALONG THE ROAD,
THOSE CHALLENGES HAS HELP YOU
DISCOVER SPECIAL GIFTS, TALENTS, AND INTERESTS.
THOSE VERY CHALLENGES CAN BE USED
TO MAKE A CONTRIBUTION TO THIS WORLD.
NO, IT HAS NOT BEEN EASY
HE NEVER SAID IT WOULD BE.
BUT HE DID PROMISE THIS, AND THAT IS,
HE WOULD NEVER LEAVE NOR FORSAKE YOU.
YOU ARE NOT HERE BY ACCIDENT **WOMAN**.
YOU ARE HERE FOR A REASON.
YOUR VERY EXISTENCE MATTERS.
SIMPLY, YOU ARE **CHOSEN**.
NOW, DUST YOUR HEELS OFF
GET OUT OF THAT PROSTRATE POSITION
GET UP, AND
STAND WOMAN STAND!

CHAPTER ONE

~ FAITH IT! ~

FAITH - /NOUN/

A word (other than a pronoun)
used to identify any of a class of people,
places, or things (common noun),
or to name a particular
one of these (proper noun).

FAITH IT!

KNOW BEYOND
A SHADOW OF DOUBT
WHEN YOU TRUST GOD
HE WILL WORK IT OUT!

WITHOUT HESITATION
NO, IF, AND, NOR BUT'S
THERE IS NOTHING TO PONDER ABOUT
NO QUESTIONING, WHAT?

SO, BELIEVE WHAT YOU SAY
AND SAY WHAT YOU MEAN
NO COMPROMISING
NO IN BETWEEN

STAND FIRM WOMAN
STOP SWAYING LIKE A LEAF
IT'S YOUR CALL
YOUR PERSONAL BELIEF

LISTEN,
YOU WILL MAKE IT!
YES, YOU CAN TAKE IT
NO NEED TO FAKE IT
SIMPLY **FAITH IT!**

I FOUND ME

COVERED UP
HIDDEN FROM MYSELF
I DISCOVERED
THIS WOMAN OF WEALTH

LIKE A CATERPILLAR
FINALLY, OUT IT'S COCOON
METAMORPHOSIS TOOK PLACE
NOT A MINUTE TOO SOON

I WAS ALWAYS THERE
JUST TUCKED AWAY
FOR THAT PERFECT MOMENT
ON THE PERFECT DAY

NOW THAT I HAVE ARRIVED
WOMAN, LADY, GIRL
I'M COVERED IN THE BLOOD
ON ASSIGNMENT FOR THE WORLD

ANOINTED AND BLESSED
FROM HEAD TO TOE
WHEREVER HE LEADS
I WILL FOLLOW

I FINALLY FOUND ME
OH YES, IT TOOK AWHILE
FOR ME TO REALIZE
I AM HIS CHOSEN CHILD

REFLECTION

WHO IS THAT?
STARING AT ME
A FACE I CAN'T DEFINE
FILLED WITH OBSCURITY

THE WOMAN IN THE MIRROR
WHERE DID SHE COME FROM?
INJURED BY LIFE
A BIT FLAWED AND NUMB

CHALLENGES OF LIFE
HAVE ALL SET IN
THE WOMAN IN THE MIRROR
CAN NO LONGER PRETEND

FACE TO FACE
SHE MUST REALIZE
HER KEY TO HAPPINESS
LIES DEEP INSIDE

WITH A STRONG DESIRE
TO BE SET FREE
THAT WOMAN IN THE MIRROR
COULD SHE BE ME?

DON'T STAY IN THE ASHES

Crawl out

Walk out

Run Out

Come out!

WOMAN!

You've been down there too long

Get out of the rubbish

Don't give way to the mess

CHILE!!!

Stop Worrying

And start Worshipping!

Get your stuff back!

I know…

Life feels like a thief

That crept up and robbed you

Of Your Essence

Your Joy

Your Peace

Your Mind

Your You!

When life gets tough

Don't stray!

Simply, pray…

God will give you **BEAUTY**

For those **ASHES**

Now get up **GIRL!**

And wash your **FACE!**

GRACE SAID NO!

Grace is the Star
Of my story
Let me tell you about
To whom I give the GLORY!

Satan's been after me
Because of whom I serve
Trying to take me out
He really has the nerve

Suddenly,
Like a thief in the night
Him and his minions
Tried to take my life

As I gasped for air
Was I history?
Is this it?
Lord, what's happening to me?

Haven't finished the assignment
There's still too much to do
Help me Lord!
I can't do this without You

But Grace stepped in
To death, it said NO!
Blew life back into me
And opened up the door

I'm back on assignment
Shouting to and fro
Telling the world about Jesus
Everywhere I go!

His Grace truly is Sufficient…

DIAMOND IN THE ROUGH

IT'S TIME...
TO STEP OUTSIDE THE BOX
TRUST MYSELF
LIVE TODAY
AS IF IT'S MY LAST

IT'S TIME...
TO BELIEVE
I REALLY CAN DO ALL THINGS
THROUGH CHRIST WHO STRENGTHENS ME

IT'S TIME...
TO STOP CRYING
LOOKING FOR A SHOULDER
OR SOMEONE TO TELL ME
IT'S GOING TO BE OKAY

IT'S TIME
TO DIG DEEPER...
EVEN IN THE DRY PLACES OF MY LIFE
AND BELIEVE THAT SOON
I WILL DISCOVER BURIED TREASURE

IT'S TIME...
TO SNATCH MY LIFE BACK
OUT OF THE CLUTCHES OF MAN
AND FORGIVE...
THE WOMAN IN THE MIRROR
AND ACKNOWLEDGE
SHE TRULY IS A **DIAMOND**

ME

PRETENDED TO LIKE ME
TRIED…
TO DRAIN ME

YEAH, YOU USED ME
SECRETLY…
TRIED TO STAIN ME

WHY DO YOU ENVY ME
SIMPLY,
WANT TO BE ME

SO,
AGAINST ME
YOU REPRESENT NEGATIVITY

I 'VE BEEN IN MY OWN LANE
ON MY OWN MISSION
TELL ME WHAT'S UP
WHY THE COMPETITION?

LIFE IS TOO SHORT
WITH ENOUGH OF IT'S TROUBLE'S
SO, GET YOURSELF TOGETHER
AND STOP LIVING IN THAT BUBBLE

I WONDER

I WONDER WHAT IT'S LIKE
TO BASK IN THE BLISS
FEEL COMPLETE
MY LOVE NOT REMISS

I WONDER WHAT IT'S LIKE
TO ANTICIPATE THE SENSATION
THAT WHEN WE ARE TOGETHER
IT'S ALWAYS A CELEBRATION

I WONDER WHAT IT'S LIKE
TO BE THE APPLE OF SOMEONE'S EYE
WILL I EVER KNOW THIS FEELING
BEFORE I DIE

I WONDER WHAT IT'S LIKE
TO EXPERIENCE RECIPROCITY
KNOWING THE LOVE IS MUTUAL
NO QUESTION OF SECURITY

I WONDER WHAT IT'S LIKE
TO ENCOUNTER AGELESS LOVE
ENSURED BY HIS EMBRACE
HE WAS SENT FROM ABOVE

I REALLY DO WONDER
IF ANY OF THIS IS IDEAL
OR AM I BLINDED BY CLICHE'
AND REAL LOVE IS SURREAL

I DO WONDER...

SHEROE'

WHAT KIND…
OF WOMAN IS THIS?
HELL HAS NO FURY
LIFE HAS NO BLISS

BORN TO FIGHT
STRONG, BOLD, AND WISE
THE GIFT OF LONG-SUFFERING
HAS BEEN HER PRIZE

DISCOLORED…
PAIN IS HER NAME
EXCLUSIVELY CHOSEN
TO BEAR LIFE STAINS

SHEROE'
PRIDE TRIES TO BREAK HER DOWN
CONSPIRING AND PLOTTING
DESIRING HER CROWN

YOU FIGHT ON WOMAN
BLESSED FROM ABOVE
TRULY YOU'RE SYMBOLIC
OF HIS AMAZING LOVE

WOMAN OF GOD

BOLD, BRAVE
BEAUTIFUL, BLESSED
CALLED ACCORDING TO PURPOSE
SET APART FROM THE REST

WOMAN OF GOD
STANDING ON THE FRONT LINE
WARRIOR OF THE WORD
REPRESENTING THE DIVINE

SPIRITUAL AND STRONG
YET, SWEET TO THE SOUL
WISE ENOUGH TO KNOW
WHO'S TOTALLY IN CONTROL

GIRDED UP IN ARMOR
READY COME WHAT MAY
FILLED WITH THE ANOINTING
TO CHASE DEMONS AWAY

AN HEIR TO THE THRONE
A QUEEN SHE'S PERCEIVED
NO MATTER WHERE SHE GOES
SHE EXEMPLIFY ROYALTY

WOMAN OF GOD
LOYAL TO THE END
FULFILLING DESTINY
STANDING AGAINST THE WIND

BE ENCOURAGED

SOMETIMES IT'S ALL
SEEMS JUST TOO MUCH
YOU FEEL AS IF
YOU HAVE NOTHING BUT BAD LUCK

WHEN YOUR DREAMS AND VISIONS
ALL SEEM TO TARRY
THOSE HEAVY BURDENS
ARE TOO MUCH TO CARRY

BE ENCOURAGED
YOU HAVE A FRIEND
THAT WILL STAND BY YOUR SIDE
THROUGH THICK AND THIN

HE IS A ROCK
IN A WEARY LAND
GAVE HIS SON
TO SAVE ALL MAN

SO, BE ENCOURAGED
NO NEED TO DOUBT
NO MATTER WHAT THE PROBLEM
GOD WILL WORK IT OUT!

OPEN MY HEART

CAN I TRUST YOU
IF I GIVE YOU MY HEART
HANDLE IT WITH CARE
FROM THE VERY START?

WILL YOU PRESERVE IT
LIKE FRUIT IN A JAR?
CAN YOU LIGHT IT UP
LIKE THE MORNING STAR?

FOR IT HAS BEEN BROKEN
CRUSHED AND FRAYED TOO
TOSSED FROM SIDE TO SIDE
CHANGED FROM RED TO BLUE

IT DESIRES TRUE LOVE
AND CRIES OUT FOR JOY
TO BE TREATED TENDERLY
NOT PLAYED LIKE A TOY

CAN I REALLY TRUST YOU
IF I LET YOU IN?
WILL YOU BE REAL
AND NOT PRETEND?

SHOULD I TAKE A CHANCE
ON YOU TREATING ME RIGHT
FULFILLING MY EVERYTHING
MORNING, NOON AND NIGHT?

DON'T KNOW IF I CAN TRUST YOU
OR BE ABLE TO EXHALE
I REALLY DO WANT TO
BUT TIME WILL ONLY TELL

~RELECTIONS~

1. Which poetic piece in this chapter spoke to you and why?

2. Knowing your and the writers' journey, what resonates with you most from that piece?

3. After reading this entire chapter, what keywords strengthen you to STAND?

4. What in this chapter gave you something to think about?

5. How would this chapter benefit you after reading it?

CHAPTER TWO
~COURAGE~

WHEN THE STORM IS RAGING

THE STIRRING OF THE WIND
DOWN-POUR OF THE RAIN
THIS STORM THAT I'M IN
IS A WHIRLWIND OF PAIN

AROUND AND AROUND
FEELS LIKE A TORNADO
HOLDING ON FOR LIFE
NOT KNOWING IF I'M ABLE

THUNDER AND LIGHTNING
AS TREACHEROUS AS CAN BE
THESE CARES OF LIFE
ARE GETTING THE BEST OF ME

OH, THIS IS A BAD ONE
LORD INTERFERE
THE WAY THAT IT'S LOOKING
THIS MAY NEVER CLEAR

AFTER AWHILE
THINGS START TO DIE DOWN
THE RAIN SUBSIDES
AND SETTLE ON THE GROUND

GRADUALLY THE SUN
PEEK OUT IT'S PLACE OF SLUMBER
REPLACING THE DIMNESS
AND FORECAST I WAS UNDER

YES, LIFE STORMS
WILL COME AND GO
BUT GOD WILL DELIVER
FOR THIS I SURELY KNOW

BATTLE SCARS

BLEMISHED BEYOND
THE NAKED EYE
MY BATTLE SCARS
I NO LONGER HIDE

PROUDLY WORN
FOR THE WORLD TO SEE
I'M STILL HERE
JUST A BETTER ME

BADGES OF COURAGE
MEDALS OF FAITH
AWARDED ANOTHER CHANCE
TO FINISH THE RACE

THESE SCARS...
I NOW PROCLAIM
NEVER GIVING ACCEPTANCE
TO BEING LABELED STAINED

THANK YOU, FATHER
WHAT YOU'VE DONE FOR ME
THE BATTLE HAS BEEN WON
I AM CANCER FREE!

SURVIVORS

Strong and brave
Fighters each one
Been to Hell and back
To cancer, they didn't succumb

From every situation
And every walk of life
Woman Warriors
Truly paid the price

Soldiers in the Army
Standing on the front line
A little shattered, not broken
Simply, one-of-a-kind

So AMAZING!
Highly favored and blessed
These Survivors
Are withstanding the test

The gaze in their eyes
Oh, such a beautiful sight!
KEEP STANDING STRONG WOMAN!
Day will replace the night

RECOVERY

TUBES AND NEEDLES
ATTACHED TO ME
BODY ON DISPLAY
AS I LAY IN RECOVERY

OPENING MY EYES
NUMB, FEELING NO PAIN
I WANTED TO KNOW
WHAT PARTS OF ME REMAIN

SOMETHING HAPPEN
DURING THE SURGERY
SOMEHOW DEEP WITHIN
I KNEW I WAS CANCER-FREE

YOU'RE GOING TO BE OKAY
SAID THE DOCTOR IN CHARGE
ASSURING ME THAT MY RECOVERY
WOULDN'T BE THAT HARD

GOD, I THANK YOU
FOR LOVING ME SO MUCH
YOU SAVED MY LIFE
SIMPLY, WITH YOUR TOUCH

RESCUE ME

LIKE ROLLING WATER
TOSSED SIDE TO SIDE
I'M IN NEED OF A NAVIGATOR
TO BE MY GUIDE

THIS HERE WATER
IS TOO DEEP
THROW ME A LIFELINE
I CAN'T COMPETE

THE ROUGH TIDES
AND UNSETTLED WIND
I CALL FOR AN ANCHOR
TO PULL ME IN

FOR I AM WEARY
TIRED OF THE HOLD
FATHER, I SURRENDER
MIND, BODY, AND SOUL

I'M SLOWLY SINKING
PLEASE DON'T LET ME DROWN
RESCUE ME LORD!
I KNOW YOU'RE STILL AROUND

DELAYED, NOT DENIED

DON'T GIVE UP
IT'S ON THE WAY
DON'T YOU LISTEN
TO WHAT OTHER'S SAY

IT'S COMING…
GOD IS WORKING IT OUT
CLEARING ALL THE MESS
THAT'S STIRRING ABOUT

LISTEN…
ONE THING HE WON'T DO
HE WILL NEVER LIE
NOR ABANDON YOU

IT'S YOURS
NO ONE CAN TAKE IT AWAY
JUST TRUST IN GOD
AND CONTINUE TO PRAY

DELAYED
DOESN'T MEAN DENIED
STAND IN YOUR FAITH
AND STOP QUESTIONING, WHY?

NEW SKIN

THIS SKIN I'M IN
HAS STARTED TO SHED
PEELING AWAY EXCESS
THINGS THAT ARE DEAD

A NEW COVERING
HAS REPLACED THE OLD
AN UNEXPLAINABLE GLOW
LOOK GOOD I'M TOLD

THAT OLD SKIN I WAS IN
WAS VULNERABLE AND WEAK
BLEMISHED BY LIFE
IT WAS TOO MEEK

THAT DAY CAME
I SAID ENOUGH IS ENOUGH
I DECIDED TO CHANGE
MY SKIN BECAME TOUGH

OH, I LOOK SPLENDID
INSIDE AND OUT
ONLY GOD REALLY KNOWS
WHAT THIS IS ABOUT

LOOK AT ME NOW
DO YOU LIKE WHAT YOU SEE?
I'M OUT MY COCOON
I'M A BRAND-NEW ME

GIVE ME A REASON

WHAT?
AM I HERE FOR
I FOLLOWED
THE GOLDEN RULE
WHY?
DO I CONSTANTLY LOSE
MY FATE STUCK
BETWEEN A ROCK
AND HARD PLACE
WHEN?
DO I WIN
NO LONGER
CAN I PRETEND
IS THIS THE END?
HOW?
DID I GET HERE
DELIRIOUS
I'M SO SERIOUS
ENOUGH IS ENOUGH!
I'M JUST NOT THAT TOUGH
WHERE?
IS LOVE
JOY
PEACE
THE MORNING STAR

THEY DON'T
VISIT ME ANYMORE
IT'S SO GLOOMY
GIVE ME A REASON
TO NOT END
THIS…
BUT WAIT…
THERE IS HOPE!
A SILVER LINING!
A RIBBON IN THE SKY!
A BETTER TOMORROW!
A GOD THAT TRULY
LOVES ME
NO MATTER WHAT
I NOW UNDERSTAND
AND KNOW
THE REASON…

FAITH

THANK YOU, LORD,
FOR BLESSING ME
IN THE MIDST OF IT ALL
I GOT THE VICTORY

THAT OLE' BATTLE
WAS NEVER MINE
ONCE I TURNED IT OVER
IT WORKED OUT FINE

I STOOD STILL
CONTINUED TO PRAY
YOU KNEW THE DEAL
BECAUSE YOU ARE THE WAY

I'VE LEARNED TO TRUST YOU
SURRENDER ALL MY CARES
YOU FREED ME UP
NO MORE BURDENS TO SHARE

NEVER AGAIN
I'LL TRY TO WORK IT OUT
I NOW UNDERSTAND
WHAT FAITH IS ABOUT

~RELECTIONS~

1. Which poetic piece in this chapter spoke to you and why?

2. Knowing your and the writers' journey, what resonates with you most from that piece?

3. After reading this entire chapter, what keywords strengthen you to STAND?

4. What in this chapter gave you something to think about?

5. How would this chapter benefit you after reading it?

CHAPTER 3

~RESILIENT~

THIS WON'T BREAK ME!

STAND TALL AS A TOWER
STRONG AS ROARING SEAS
THIS SITUATION
WILL NOT BREAK ME!

EVERYTHING
SEEMS OUT OF CONTROL
I WON'T GIVE IN
I WILL STAND BOLD

THOSE FIERY DARTS
THAT'S BEEN CAST MY WAY
WILL NOT PENETRATE
YOU UNDERSTAND WHAT I SAY?

IT MAY FORM
BUT IT WON'T PROSPER
I'M THE HEAD NOT THE TAIL
AND THAT IS THE GOSPEL!

THIS WON'T BREAK ME
I WILL PERSEVERE
MY GOD HASN'T GIVEN ME
THE SPIRIT OF FEAR
THIS WON'T BREAK ME!

PUSHED!

WHEN ALL ELSE FAILS
WITH NO STRENGHT TO FIGHT
SURROUNDED BY DARKNESS
DON'T SEE ANY LIGHT

LOST…
NOT SURE WHICH WAY TO GO
DUCKING AND DODGING
ALL OF THOSE BLOWS

PUSHED BEYOND LIMIT
BARELY CATCH YOUR BREATH
STAGGERING AND STUMBLING
LORD, SEND ME SOME HELP

DESPERATE FOR RELIEF
PRAYING FOR AN END
TO ALL OF THE HELL
YOU'VE BEEN WALLOWING IN

BUT ALL OF A SUDDEN
YOU REALIZE
YOU HAVE AN ANCHOR
WHO'S BY YOUR SIDE
NO MATTER WHAT
YOU GOTTA PUSH THROUGH!

IF THEY ONLY KNEW

While they murmur
You keep moving
Lashes of tainted words
Spewed…
Trying to inflict harm
Upon you
If they only knew… the woman you are

Their tongue
The meanest member
Possessed with venom
Intentionally, try to destroy you
If they only knew…the woman you are

The chattering of destructive words
Snakingly slither
From their slanderous mouth
Hoping to gain an alliance to join their nest
If they only knew… the woman you are

An attempted assassination
Irrelevant noise
Spreading rumors
Of mass destruction
Spilling from their lips
If they only knew...the woman you are

Listen woman!
Your ears are not a garbage can
Don't receive the trash
Let them hate!
You continue to be great!
They just don't care to know…
The woman you are

GOING THROUGH

HERE WE GO!
HE'S AT IT AGAIN
THAT EVIL SCOUNDREL
ISN'T MY FRIEND

EVIL ONE
PLOTTING HIS NEXT ATTACK
TRYING TO FIND A WAY
TO THROW ME OFF TRACK

UP AND DOWN
LIKE A ROLLERCOASTER RIDE
IT'S HARD TO BELIEVE
I'M STILL ALIVE

I WILL FIND A WAY
TO PERSEVERE
I WASN'T BORN
WITH THE SPIRIT OF FEAR

NO MATTER WHAT
UNTIL MY LAST BREATH
HE IS MY SAVIOR
MY PRESENT HELP

I WON'T QUIT

IT'S BEEN SO HARD
DON'T KNOW WHAT TO DO
NO ONE COULD EVER
WALK IN THESE SHOES

BLISTERED AND BRUISED
TRYING TO FIND MY WAY
PRESSING ON
STRUGGLING NOT TO STRAY

DO I GO EAST
WHEN THE SIGN POINTS WEST?
I'M IN NEED OF A GUIDE
TO HELP ME OUT THIS MESS

STRENGHTEN ME!
I'M ON SHAKY GROUND
WALK WITH ME LORD
I KNOW YOU'RE STILL AROUND

THROUGH IT ALL
NO MATTER WHAT
I STILL…
WON'T QUIT!

FIGHT!

IT'S IN ME
THE WILL TO FIGHT
ENOUGH OF THIS MESS
I KNOW MY RIGHTS

TO BE HAPPY
FOREVER FREE
THRIVE IN MY BEING
TO SIMPLY BE ME

WITH EVERY KNOCK DOWN
I'LL RISE AGAIN
BACK IN THE RING
DETERMINE TO WIN

BRUISED AND BATTERED
A WOUND HERE OR THERE
I WON'T GIVE UP
THIS I SWEAR

SO, BRING IT ON
I'M COVERED IN THE BLOOD
I AM CHAMPION
AN INSTRUMENT OF GOD'S LOVE

HE KEPT ME

STRUGGLE AFTER STRUGGLE
DEFEAT ON TOP OF DEFEAT
TRIALS AND TRIBULATIONS
HAVE ALL MADE ME WEAK

THROUGH EVERY SITUATION
AND CIRCUMSTANCE OF LIFE
I REMEMBER THE BLOOD
I WON'T FORGET THE PRICE

HE IS MY REFUGE
ONE THAT I CAN CLAIM
I'M STANDING ON HIS WORD
AND IT HAS KEPT ME SANE

I'M HIS CHOSEN VESSEL
THE ONE HE SAVED
BECAUSE OF HIS TOUCH
I'M STRONG, BOLD, AND BRAVE

YES, HE KEPT ME
TIME AND TIME AGAIN
I WILL TRUST HIM
WITH THAT I'M SURE TO WIN

IT WILL BE ALRIGHT

TRIED AND TRIED
GAVE EVERYTHING WITHIN
HOPING, PRAYING, STAYING
LIVING IN PRETEND

PUTTING UP A FRONT
PERFORMANCES AND ACTS
LIFE IS TOO SHORT
WON'T YOU FACE THE FACTS

YOUR CUP IS ALMOST EMPTY
YOU'VE POURED OUT ENOUGH
TAKE A STAND WOMAN
IT'S IN YOU TO BE TOUGH!

GRAB YOUR BAG
STOP LIVING IN LACK
SHIFT UNTIL DESTINY
AND DON'T DARE LOOK BACK!

DEAD WEIGHT

WHY YOU CARRY
ALL THAT DEAD WEIGHT?
IT'S TIME TO RELEASE IT
BEFORE IT'S TOO LATE

AREN'T YOU TIRED
OF THAT LOAD
BARELY HOLDING YOURSELF UP
IF THE TRUTH BE TOLD

THAT EXTRA BAGGAGE
IS WEIGHING YOU DOWN
IF YOU KEEP ON LUGGING IT
YOU MAY NOT BE AROUND

IT DOESN'T BELONG TO YOU
NOW, GIVE IT BACK!
RETURN IT TO SENDER
AS-A MATTER OF FACT

YOU GOT YOUR OWN ISSUES
TO DEAL WITH
ENOUGH IS ENOUGH
IT'S TIME YOU QUIT

NOW, MOVE ON
YOU DESERVE A BREAK
SIMPLY GET RID OF
ALL THAT DEAD WEIGHT

ANOINT ME!

SOMETIMES A DIP
JUST WON'T DO
YOU NEED A POURING
OF HIS ANOINTING ON YOU

WONDERNG WHY
SO MUCH PAIN
FEELING AS IF
YOU HAVE NOTHING TO GAIN

BROKEN AND BATTERED
HUMILIATED AN SHAME
LIED AND CHEATED ON
FEELING ALMOST INSANE

STRETCHED BEYOND LIMIT
ON SHAKEY GROUND
SOMETIMES WONDERING
IF HE IS STILL AROUND

YOU SAY I HAVE NOT
BECAUSE I DON'T ASK
SO, IN THE NAME OF THE SON
HELP ME WITH THIS TASK

I JUST GOT TO TRUST YOU
THERE IS NO OTHER CHOICE
IN THIS SEASON
I ONLY NEED TO HEAR YOUR VOICE

STAND DOWN!

LURKING IN THE DARKNESS
SEARCHING FOR SOULS
YOU EVIL SCOUNDREL
YOU ARE EXPOSED!

ENEMY OF THE LIGHT
PROWLING UP AND DOWN
IN THE NAME OF THE FATHER
IT'S TIME YOU STAND DOWN!

KILL, STEAL, AND DESTROY
IS YOUR ULTIMATE GOAL
YOU'VE BEEN DEFEATED
SO LET GOD'S PEOPLE GO!

STAND DOWN DEVIL!
YOU THINK YOU ARE SO TOUGH
YOUR DAYS ARE NUMBERED
ENOUGH IS ENOUGH

I STAND UP FOR JESUS!
TRUTH AND RIGHTEOUSNESS
NOW YOU AND ALL YOU MINIONS
RETURN TO YOUR MESS!

NARC…

YOU PLAYED THE VICTIM
AS IF I CAUSED THE PAIN
MAN IN THE MIRROR
YOU ARE LITERALLY INSANE

LOVE ME TO HATE ME
A MASTER OF DESTRUCTION
NOT WILLING TO LISTEN
TO ANYONE'S INSTRUCTION

UNSTABLE…
IS YOUR MIDDLE NAME
TORMENTING OTHERS
LEAVING YOUR DESPICABLE STAIN

A THORN IN ONES SIDE
IT'S TIME YOU DEPART
NO MORE OF YOUR STUPID GAMES
NO BREAKING OF MY HEART

NARCISSIST…
GOOD-BYE TO FOREVER
AT THE END OF THE DAY
POTENTIALLY, YOU ARE THE DEVIL
BYE!

IT'S COPASETIC

IT'S ALL GOOD
YOU LIED
YOU MISTREATED ME
YOU HUMILIATED AND DECEIVED ME
YOU JUST PLAINLY
DIDN'T DO RIGHT
BY ME
BUT IT'S ALL GOOD
IT'S YOUR LOST
YOU SEE…
I'M A GOOD, KIND, LOVING, WOMAN
I AM THE SEVEN'S
OF GOD'S CRAFTSMANSHIP
I AM SAGE, SASSY, SENSUAL, SOULFUL, SPIRITUAL
SENSATIONAL AND MOST OF ALL
SAVED!
I WANT YOU TO KNOW
IT WAS NEVER ABOUT YOU
IT'S ALL ABOUT HIM
SO, WITH ALL UNDUE RESPECT
OR THAT WATER THANG!
YOU DON'T MISS YOUR WATER
UNTIL YOUR WELL RUNS DRY
I GUESS YOU BETTER GO FIND
ANOTHER WATERFALL
BECAUSE TRULY IT IS, **COPASETIC!**

STAGES

THERE ARE THREE STAGES
IN YOUR WALK WITH CHRIST
EACH ONE HAS IT'S PURPOSE
SEPARATELY IT'S PRICE

THE FIRST IS BIRTH
A PERIOD OF GESTATION
A TIME TO LEARN
A PHASE OF EDIFICATION

THE SECOND IS CRISIS
A SEASON OF LOTS OF PAIN
SOMETIMES SO DIFFICULT
MERE WORDS CAN'T EXPLAIN

BUT HOLD ON!
THERE'S ONE MORE TO GO
WHEN YOU STAND ON HIS PROMISES
BLESSINGS ARE SURE TO OVERFLOW

HERE COMES STAGE THREE!
RESTORATION NOW IN PLAY
GOD RELEASED HIS PROMISES
HE SAID HE WOULD ONE DAY

EACH OF THESE STAGES
YOU MUST GO THROUGH
IT'S PART OF THE PROCESS
SO, HE CAN USE YOU

~RELECTIONS~

1. Which poetic piece in this chapter spoke to you and why?

2. Knowing your and the writers' journey, what resonates with you most from that piece?

3. After reading this entire chapter, what keywords strengthen you to STAND?

4. What in this chapter gave you something to think about?

5. How would this chapter benefit you after reading it?

CHAPTER FOUR
~HOPE~

I BELIEVE

YOU GAVE ME HOPE
FOR A BETTER TOMORROW
COMFORT AND SUPPORTED ME
DURING MY DEEPEST SORROW

SPOKE INTO MY SPIRIT
LIFTED ME OUT OF DESPAIR
CHANGED MY LIFE
WITH YOUR TENDER LOVING CARE

I'VE WAITED…
SO VERY LONG
FOR THAT SPECIAL SOMEONE
TO COME ALONG

IT'S HARD TO BELIEVE
THAT ONE STILL EXIST
MAKE ME THINK ABOUT
THE GOOD THINGS THAT I'VE MISSED

YOU ARE CHOSEN
MADE PERFECTLY FOR ME
I PRAY THIS TIME
IT LAST UNTIL ETERNITY

FAVOR

OOPS! I'M SMILING
WHAT'S COME OVER ME?
IT'S BEEN SO LONG
AM I FINALLY FREE?

THIS IS SO JUVENILE
LISTEN, I GOTTA SHARE
I FEEL SO GIDDY AND WARM
I'M WALKING ON AIR

MY INNER BEING SPEAKS
TO NOT SETTLE FOR LESS
WHAT GOD'S DONE FOR ME
TRULY IS THE BEST

IT'S HIS FAVOR
THAT'S FALLEN ON ME
I'M SINGING AND DANCING
CAN THIS REALLY ME?

THAT THE FAMINE IS OVER
RESTORATION NOT IN PLAY
GOD RELEASED HIS PROMISES
HE SAID HE WOULD ONE DAY

FAVOR, FAVOR, FAVOR
GOD HAS GIVEN E
THINGS ARE BETTER NOW
HIS GRACE HAS SET ME FREE!

ANGEL IN DISGUISE

SITTING…
ACROSS FROM ME
DRAPED IN WHITE
WAS A MYSTERY
COVERED,
FROM HEAD TO TOE
I REALLY NEEDED TO KNOW

WAS HE AN ANGEL IN DISGUISE?

STARING
DEEP INTO HIS EYES
I KNEW THEN
THIS WASN'T A JOKE
AS HE SPOKE
SAYING… HIS FLIGHT
HAD BEEN DELAYED
IN THE MOST SOOTHING WAY
WAS THIS A DIVINE SETUP
IN THE MOST UNIQUE WAY?

WAS HE AN ANGEL IN DISGUISE?

I FELT COMPOSE
TO ASK A FEW QUESTIONS
THROUGH WORDS OF FAITH
WE MADE
A SPIRITUAL CONNECTION
SHARED WORDS
ABOUT HIS LIFE
DENIED HIS LIFE
DYING TO THE WORLD
MADE THE ULTIMATE SACRIFICE
TO SERVE GOD WHOLELY

WAS HE AN ANGEL IN DISGUISE?

HIS FAVORITE SCRIPTURE
WAS TO NOT RUN
OR LABOR IN VAIN
THAT SERVING CHRIST
ETERNITY
WILL BE YOUR GAIN
I WILL NEVER FORGET
HOW HE MADE ME FEEL

THIS ANGEL IN DISGUISE
TRULY IS THE REAL DEAL…

I FEEL GOOD

I FEEL GOOD TODAY
THIS IS RARE
BEEN SO BURDEN DOWN
I'M FINALLY COMING UP FOR AIR

ACTUALLY CONTENT
NO AIRS DO I PUT ON
IN FACT, I AM HAPPY
YESTERDAY CARES ARE GONE

I DO WONDER
WHERE THIS WILL LEAD
IT'S NOT OFTEN
I'M ABLE TO BREATHE

ABSORBING EVERY MOMENT
TOMORROW, I DON'T KNOW
THINGS MAY BE DIFFERENT
I HAVE THE PAST TO SHOW

FOR NOW, I'LL ENJOY
WHAT'S BEEN CAST MY WAY
RELISHING EVERY MOMENT
AND CONTINUING TO PRAY
I FEEL GOOD!

ENLARGE MY TERRITORY

BLESS ME, FATHER,
GRANT MY REQUEST
HONOR ME LIKE JABEZ
GIVE ME THE BEST

REMEMBER MY HEART
AND PERSERVERANCE TOO
SEARCH ME, LORD
THROUGH AND THROUGH

I MAY NOT BE WORTHY
OR HONORABLE AS JABEZ
BUT I AM YOUR VESSEL
WITHOUT YOU I WON'T LAST

ONLY YOU HAVE THE POWER
TO GRANT THIS DECREE
SHOWER DOWN GRACE
AND INCREASE MY NEEDS

HEARKEN TO MY CRY
HEAR MY PLEA
BASED ON MY HEART
ENLARGE MY TERRITORY

ALL IS FORGIVEN

It is truly AMAZING how time heals all things
From an open wound to a shattered heart
Time is the best remedy
With time, I have to move on to the next
I will forget what's over my shoulder
I will relinquish any attached emotions
I FORGIVE YOU…
Deep down inside
I believe you cared and tried
I FORGIVE YOU…
But, most of all, deep down
I know you loved me
In your own special way
I FORGIVE YOU…
You know God gave His only son to die for us
And despite how we've treated Him
He forgives us
I pray one day, the blinders come off, and you see
Who the enemy really is
I also pray that complete deliverance comes your way
But most of all, I pray that you believe
I always had your best interest
You probably won't believe what I'm saying
But it doesn't matter anymore
ALL IS FORGIVEN
Lastly, I pray one day,
You'll forgive me, to

IT IS WELL…

WHEN ALL IS SAID AND DONE
TO LIFE CARES, I WILL NOT SUCCUMB
I MUST GIVE WAY TO GOD
FROM THE VERY DEPTHS OF MY HEART
IT IS WELL…

WON'T DEPEND ON MAN
TO BE MY HELPING HAND
IN HIM, I PUT ALL MY TRUST
NO NEED TO PUT UP A FUSS
IT IS WELL…

STOP TRYING TO FIGURE IT OUT
HE ALREADY KNOW'S WHAT IT'S ABOUT
SURRENDER EVERY CARE
FROM THIS DAY ON, I SWEAR
IT IS WELL…

I LAY ALL AT HIS THRONE
WHEN I 'M FEELING SO ALONE
THERE WILL BE A BETTER TOMORROW
EVEN IN MY DEEPEST SORROW
IT IS WELL…
IT IS WELL…
WITH MY SOUL…

~RELECTIONS~

1. Which poetic piece in this chapter spoke to you and why?

2. Knowing your and the writers' journey, what resonates with you most from that piece?

3. After reading this entire chapter, what keywords strengthen you to STAND?

4. What in this chapter gave you something to think about?

5. How would this chapter benefit you after reading it?

CHAPTER 5

~GUEST POETS~

WORTHY
by: Nicole Walker

Hey Queen!
Who gave you permission
To take your crown off??

Who told you
That it was okay to relinquish
Your God-given state?

Some days
It may seem heavy to bear
And other days
You may not seem worthy of it

But God chose you!
To carry such a mantle
Because he knew
You were deserving of it

Now pick up your crown
And walk…
With your head held high
Knowing
That you are everything
That God has called
You to be
You are…**Royalty**

HOPE
by: Tracy Adside

I see the setting of the sun

On your strength…

They say once grown

Twice a child

The labor of your love for us

Keeps you fighting

Our love for you

Won't give up the hope

The great hope

That awaits

Keeps our hearts in faith

Your voice

I have learned to cherish

Because I know someday

It will be a distant memory

Do what you can

While you can

You said so many times

So, I choose to love you
And honor you
Because…
There is only one you
The legacy and the magic
Of life is but a vapor
I hold my breath
So that your flickering flame
Never quenches

ADDICTED

by: Stephania Perkins Biddings

Pain, Blame, Shame
Were all her drugs of choice
She never knew what thriving was
As she never found her voice
No one ever heard her cries
'Cause she never shared a sound
On her knees in pain, she'd pray
Her voice forever bound

Pain became her comfort
And even a welcome friend
--One she could rely on
And find comfort from within
Numb to blame and shame
She cared less where they rested
Struggle was a common resource
In that she seemed invested

But at night she'd click her heels
Traveling to distant lands
--Never knowing the power to live and thrive
Lay right within her hands…

I AM
by: Merrel Plet

Why am I still here?

This is going through my mind

My heart

Through the essence of my being

Why am I going through this Pain, Despair?

My body and my skin hurt

Every fiber of my being aches

The agony is tangible

Why are my lungs still breathing?

Why is my heart still beating?

When with every breath and beat I hear

I do not want to be here

Why AM I still here?!

I **AM** created in HIS image!

HIS breath fills my lungs

HIS blood flows through my veins!

Before the beginning of time, **I AM** knew me!

I **AM** calls me, HIS child

And HE calls me HIS own!

He has HIS hand on me.

I AM placed **HIS** purpose on my life.

and that is why

I. AM. Still. Here

THE RIDE
by: Brenda Washington

BEING LET DOWN
FROM THE ONE YOU LOVE
IS NOT A LETDOWN,
IT'S A DISAPPOINTMENT
YOU BUILD THEM UP,
SO, THEY CAN LET YOU DOWN

WHAT A CONFUSION
CALLED "ROLLERCOASTER,"
UP AND DOWN GOES THE EMOTIONS
OF THIS RIDE CALLED LIFE

DO YOU ALLOW YOURSELF
TO CONTINUE TO GET ON THE RIDE
OR ARE YOU BRAVE ENOUGH
TO GET OFF?

HMMMM…

SOMETIMES IT'S FAST.
OTHER TIMES IT'S SLOW
BUT NEVERTHELESS,
IT'S A RIDE
THAT YOU'LL NEVER KNOW
IT'S SPEED,
OR WHEN IT STOPS…

SO, ASK YOURSELF,
IS THIS RIDE
COSTING YOU MORE
THEN, YOU'RE WILLING TO PAY
OR TAKE?

BE BRAVE, BE STRONG,
SAY NO MORE UP AND DOWN
AND AROUND AND AROUND!

YOU SEE,
EVERY RIDE THAT YOU GET ON
SHOULD BE
ONLY WHEN GOD IS IN CONTROL
OF THE WHEEL
YOU OWE YOURSELF
MORE THAN YOU'RE SETTLING FOR

THEY'RE NOT WORTH IT…
IT'S NOT WORTH IT…
YOU ARE TOO VALUABLE…

BE ALL THAT YOU CAN BE
BECAUSE IT'S MORE TO THIS WONDERFUL LIFE
THAN
DISAPPOINTMENT, STRIFE, AND HEARTBREAK

STOP THAT WRECKLESS RIDE
DRY YOUR TEARS…
CHOOSE YOU AND WIN!
GOD HAS
AN AWESOME DAY
FOR YOU TOMORROW
IT'S YOURS
FOR THE TAKING
ONLY IF
YOU
GET OFF THE RIDE…

SWEET SKIN...
by: Lucretia Williams

At times I've had a love/ hate relationship

With my skin

I've had to endure

Blemishes, dark spots, white spots and now wrinkles...

What's next?

As I think to myself

Why can't my skin be flawless?

My thoughts led me to products

That has helped with the process

Such as:

Scrubs, Creams and Butters

That makes it slide and glide

That smooths, softens and invigorates

To the touch

Even though the products helped

With the outer glow of my skin

The journey truly has not been easy

You see...

My way of thinking had to change

I now embrace the texture and imperfections

Of my seasoned melanated skin

I've come to realize

That I'm beautiful and more than my skin
The essence of it all is that
I had to start loving
The skin I'm in
Which has blossomed into
the **"SWEET SKIN"** that now resides within

"THE ENEMY"
by: Sherrie Clentscale

The enemy is not

Our Brothers and Sisters

We see every day

He's out to attack us

In every way...

He will attack our bodies,

Our families

And our minds

Therefore,

We must stay vigilant

At all times...

When our health is attacked;

God will either heal our bodies,

Or call us home to glory...

Either way,

There is a testimony

In our story...

In the flesh;

We are not completed

But just know...

The Enemy (SATAN) Is DEFEATED!

Fight On!
by: Rebecca Vaughns

Inhale! Exhale! Breathe!
FIGHT ON!

Sabotage makes attempts to keep you shut out
FIGHT ON!

Unexpected loss challenges your emotions
FIGHT ON!

Storms come nonstop
FIGHT ON!

Suicide tries to claim you
FIGHT ON!

Depression rides your heels hard
FIGHT ON!

Your past haunts you daily
FIGHT ON!

Darkness whispers that you'll never see light
FIGHT ON!

THE DEVIL TEST YOU 24/7 IN ALL MANNERS!!!
FIGHT ON!

You struggle Mentally, Emotionally, Physically, Spiritually,
and Fnancially

But…
FIGHT ON!

Precious Girl
by: Renee Holmes

Why did God bring her into this world?

Made her a rare woman

Gave her a heart to care

Teaching her how to see life

Through His eyes

Wisdom to recognize

Satan, when he tries to rise

God has given her strength

Along this journey

Life Way

It was God

With her, each and every day

When life sends her a blow

She stood strong

Even though life seems low

Through the fire

Like the Hebrew boys

The King of Kings

Lifted her higher

She decided to choose

So, that she would not lose

It was Jesus

Who opened her eyes and said

See…

I Am Whom

Has set you free

Oh, Precious Girl…

That's why I brought you into this world

HE'S ALWAYS NEAR
by: Dayle Hoffman

Tucked down in my belly

My secrets are swelling

Lie after lie

I am telling

Start to become compelling

This weight I am feeling

I feel as though

I am stealing

Sipping on tea and taking communion

A voice speaks out as if it's a reunion

Convicting me of the darkness within

I have committed the greatest sin

Babylon it says…

loud and clear

Boy oh boy do I start to fear

Worry and tears where do I begin

Convicted like a felon

Lord, God I repent

For I know this is Heaven sent

Making things right

I must fight with all my might

All for my good in the end it's clear

God's love He shows me

Is always near

I GOT YOU GIRL
by: Stacey C. McCoy

In the tapestry of life, so unfurled
A bond of strength, it's called "**I Got You, Girl**"
Through trails and triumphs, hand in hand we swirl
In the name of sisterhood, our precious pearl
Through the stormy nights and the bright day's whirl
We'll navigate together, dear sister, in this world
In unity and love, our flags will unfurl
For women's empowerment, let our banner swirl
With hearts ablaze, our spirits unfurl
Supporting each other, we'll conquer and twirl
In this circle of trust, we'll stand and swirl
In the name of humanity, forever our girl
Through every challenge, life's winding swirl
We'll protect, empower, our banner will twirl
In solidarity and love, our legacy we'll unfurl
For sisterhood's embrace, is our precious pearl
So, remember dear sister, in this vast world
No matter what comes, in strength we'll twirl
Hand in hand, side by side, our spirits unfurl
"I Got You Girl,"
Forever as we stand and swirl!

Still Standing
by: Chaunquavia Manuel

My breast is hurting

My faith is worthless

How can I trust you God

When I'm enduring these cancerous curses?

Pill after pill

I felt every drop of chemotherapy

But God, I can't feel you

Suicide is dancing in my head

I am so drained

God, heal me, I need you like never before

Then a voice whispers

"Give it to me daughter

Haven't I done this before

I'm trying to, but you won't open the door

Nothing new is under the sun

I need you to trust me in this process

Your healing is already done

Stop complaining and fight

Fast, Pray, and seek me at midnight
I'm here for you, and I never left
It's you that I've lost your trust, is what I never felt

I need your spiritual obedience
Love me and trust me, then your healing will be immediate
Sacrifice your time
Social media got you so blind
Fast from your phone and false prophecies
Because I need you to be one of my greatest testimonies
You shall remain standing…
Stand Woman Stand!"

I Wish –
by Sheleenya C-J

Starlight, starbright…
Why did Ma marry this octopus?
Hands all over me
Seeds planted, secret's out
This baby will never see the light of day
First star I see tonight…
Life goes on
Aaah, puppy love, so innocent and pure
Holding hands, kisses on the cheek
Candy love, is oh so sweet
Heartbreak
I wish I may…
Life goes on, Love continues
In search of the Ultimate love
Of God
There's none greater, but wait
I broke His heart
When I stepped away from my Master's plan
I wish I might…
Find true love
Man after man after man after man
This is crazy!
My Father who art in heaven
Rescue me!
Have the wish…I Wish..
My husband, My son, My God, My Love…

Check On Your Strong Friends
by: Gina 'GiGi" Mobley

Carrying the world's weight

On my shoulder

Somebody should've told me

That as I get older

People become bolder and bolder

You see, you have the givers and the takers

The ones that are the realists

And the ones that are the fakers

You see…

I was born (Ford) and built tough

Edges a little rough

I'll never stop

until I feel it's enough.

Is it enough?

Is it really enough?

Have you ever been so strong

Until you just tied

Not (tired)

But tied of being strong

You see…

I am that strong friend

You know strong friends get tired too

But I ain't never too strong

To check on me,

Boo…

Just Check

On your strong friends, friend...

STRENGTH – POWER – LOVE
by: Trivia Glaze Williams

S – **STANDING** ON THE PROMISES OF GOD
T – THE **TEST** AND TRIALS THAT WILL COME
R – **REALIZING** THAT THERE IS ONLY ONE GOD
E – **ENDURING** WHAY COMES YOUR WAY
N – KNOWING THAT GOD WILL MEET YOUR **NEEDS**
G – HIS **GRACE** IS ALWAYS SUFFICIENT
T – **TRUSTING** AND BELIEVING IN THE ALMIGHTY
H – YOUR **HELP** COMES FROM THE LORD ALWAYS

P – THERE IS **POWER** IN HIS NAME
0 – HE IS THE **ONLY** WISE GOD
W – **WILLING** TO SERVE
E – GOD IS **EVERLASTING**
R – **RENDERING** ALL TO HIM

L – **LET** GO AND **LET** GOD
O – **ONLY** GOD CAN
V – **VICTORIOUS** IS HIS NAME
E – GOD IS MY **EVERYTHING**

THERE IS STRENGTH AND POWER IN LOVE.
GOD GIVES US STRENGTH TO WALK DAILY IN POWER WITH
LOVE.
LET US LOVE ONE ANOTHER, AS GOD LOVES US

"Peace be Still"
by: Tiquana Deloach

Peace, I call you
Peace, I gave to you
Be still and know I got you

No matter how hard it gets
I am the Lord who is with you
You are not called to quit

I created you with my bare hands,
And spoke you into existence,
Masterpiece is what you are
Can't you see it?

Though the trials come, and the winds blow
The devil is already defeated
Speak my word and watch him
Back up and let you go

Don't be afraid, for I am with you
To carry you through your life's journey
Like I have always promised you

Never be intimidated by what you see
Remember it's an illusion
To get you to a place of defeat

I said Peace, I called you
Peace is your name
Be still my child
You have so much to gain.

My inheritance is all yours
You don't have to fight
Just continue to trust me
I will carry you with all my might

I am your Father in Heaven
Always have and will be
The God that answers by fire
And wins with Victory,

Remember,
Peace, I called you
Peace you shall be
Peace is your name
Be still and remain in me.
For my Peace has always been in thee.

Cancer Attack
By: Dr. Cleola Weems-Horne

Consider all the devastation that you have caused

Always popping up at the most inconvenient time

Never contemplating about the person, you attack so

ferociously

Constantly destroying the lives of individuals and their loved

ones

Evidence that you leave behind of bodies that are forever

changed

Reminding the world of your ruthlessness

CANCER, YOU SUCK!

I'M STILL STANDING
by: Denise Versatille

There are so many pieces

of me scattered

because of the pain

When will I have peace

from all these broken pieces?

I was told love and loyalty

were part of the plan

But I continuously asked myself

Why does it hurt so much?

How do I stand and weather these storms?

The Word says weeping

May endure for a night

But joy, comes in the morning

Lord, where is thy morning?

Suddenly, I heard this woman say

"STAND, WOMAN STAND!"

I questioned myself

How can I stand after all of this?

Deep down, something stirs up

Reminding me of who I serve and am

I will push, press, pray, and praise

Through…

All the hurt, pain,

Guilt, and shame!

YES!, **I'M STILL STANDING!**

ADAM AND EVE
by: Stephanie Sills

Crafty and cunning
You slithered into my life
Deceiving me with your smooth words
Without me ever thinking twice

The choice that I made
Hurt more than just me
It hurt an innocent man;
Who could this serpent be?

Adam and Eve
Lived in a perfect world
God gave one command
Never eat from the tree of good and evil.
Do you understand?

Eve went against God's wishes,
As the serpent hung from the tree
He started another conversation,
saying, Eve
…you could be smarter than God
Trust me

As he passed her the forbidden fruit,
which was pleasant to her eyes
Eve made the wrong choice,
Removing all disguise

That old serpent
Convinced her
To give it to man.
Adam, taste a little piece;
And forgot about God's plan

Delicious…
Were the words that Adam spoke
As he ate the forbidden fruit
The life they lived were soon revoked

They never should have eaten it,
They felt so ashamed
Covering up their body parts
Wondering who was the blame?

When God returned to the garden
Asked," what's going on?
Looking at each other
They tried passing the baton

It wasn't me Eve said
The snake tricked both of us
Adam shook his head and said no
It was you who put your trust

The consequence was deep
Eve, you caused so much pain
Because of you and disobedience
Woman is forever changed

Living After a Cancer Storm
by: Sabrina Cromartie, Breast Cancer Survivor

Life is a journey of struggles, storms, trials, and tribulations
God has rebirthed our journeys and replaced life's purposes
With these keys to a successful journey:
Love, Faith, Hope, Wisdom, Happiness, and Peace of Mind
Cancer Storms are created with these words intertwined:
Why?
What Did I Do?
When?
How Can I Prevent It?
Let's Advocate!
Victory!
Your Why?
Is your Love for Yourself…
Your What Did I Do?
Is your Faith…
Your When?
Is Your Hope…
Your How Can I Prevent It?
Is Your Wisdom…
Your let's Advocate!
Is Your Happiness…
Your Victory
Is your Peace of Mind…
There is Life After Cancer…

'SPECIAL TRIBUTE'

FROM A MAN'S PERSPECTIVE

"Never Her Mascara"
by: James Eagles

In the gentle dance
Of life they share
A man who loves
With the utmost care

His heart adorned
With deep respect
For the woman
He'll never "ever" neglect

He sees her strength
Her inner grace
In every line
Of her smiling face

He listens to her
Thoughts and dreams
Supporting her
In all her schemes

In every storm,
Through every trial
He stands by her
With a steadfast smile

Her tears he wipes
Her fears he soothes
She knows God leads
In what he chooses

He honors, her direction
Her voice
In him, she finds
Her safest choice

With gentle words
And patient ears
He banishes
All her darkest fears

He's the wind
Beneath her wings
Encouraging her
To chase her dreams

He builds her up
Never tears her down
In his love
She finds her solid ground

In his embrace
She knows she's free
To be herself
To just simply be

He doesn't try
To change or mold
He loves her
Young or gray and old.

With every action
With every touch
He shows his love
It means so much

Respecting her
As his equal, his friend
Their love story
One without an end

In this union
Built on trust and care
Two souls together
A true love affair

A man who provides
Loves, and protects
The woman he adores
And never forgets

In his tender touch
Her worries subside
In his loving embrace
She finds her guide

He always brings
Peace & love
But never terror
He always ruins her lipstick
But never her mascara

~RELECTIONS~

1. Which poetic piece in this book spoke to you and why?

2. Knowing your and the writers' journey, what resonates with you mostly in this book?

3. After reading this entire book, what keywords strengthen you to STAND?

4. In your deepest thoughts, how can this book help you in your breakthrough?

5. Identify one small change in your life you will make after reading this book?

CLOSING
~SIGNATURE PIECE~

THE FINISH LINE

THE FINISH LINE
YES, I MADE IT
JUST IN TIME
I FINALLY CROSS
THE FINISH LINE

THE ROADS WERE NARROW
THE HILLS VERY STEEP
PASSING THROUGH THE VALLEY
AT TIMES, I WOULD WEEP

STILL PRESSING ON
AT TIMES, TAKING A REST
NOT KNOWING WHICH DIRECTION
WOULD BE BEST

BUT LOVE SHOWED UP
GRACE MY COMPANION
FAITH STAYED AROUND
I WAS NEVER ABANDON

PEACE FLOWED ASIDE
MERCY HELD ME UP
PERSERVERANCE CHALLENGE ME
TO GET THE WINNING CUP

NOW THAT I'VE CROSSED
I AM SET FREE
FROM ALL THE BURDENS
THAT HAD ITS HOLD ON

YES, I MADE IT!
JUST IN THE NICK OF TIME!
IT FEELS REAL GOOD
TO CROSS THE FINISH LINE

'A Special Invitation'

If you have read this book and have yet to receive Jesus Christ as your Lord and Savior, I beseech you to decide right now.
It does not matter where you are and what is going on in your life.
He is waiting to receive you as you receive Him. Make Him the Lord of your life by taking the first step and saying YES. With your heart and mind fixed on Him, say this simple prayer.

**"LORD JESUS, I BELIEVE THAT YOU DIED FOR ME, AT CALVARY.
I RECEIVE YOU NOW AS MY SAVIOR AND LORD COME LIVE IN MY HEART."**

If you have said this prayer, you are now
SAVED!
Rejoice, for the Angels in heaven are rejoicing
Over your SALVATION!
Lastly, join yourself to a local body of believers
Who is preaching and teaching that Jesus is the Lord
And He is the CHRIST…

GOD BLESS!

Contact Information

If you would like to share how this book has help or encouraged you, or if you would like to consult with Valerie Allen individually for a group or organization speaking engagement/conference/professional development/workshop, etc. you can contact her at:

info@standwomanstand.org or

vgoldenallen@gmail.com

Send all correspondence to:

Stand Woman Stand, Inc.

20451 NW 2nd Avenue Suite 112

Miami Gardens, Florida 33169

Phone:786-535-9598

"DEEPEST THOUGHTS"

"DEEPEST THOUGHTS"